Prairie Spirit(s)

Rhonda Parrish

https://www.patreon.com/RhondaParrish

Publisher's Note: This is a work of fiction. Names, characters, places, and incidents are a product of the author's imagination. Locales and public names are sometimes used for atmospheric purposes. Any resemblance to actual people, living or dead, or to businesses, companies, events, institutions, or locales is completely coincidental.

Book Layout © 2014 BookDesignTemplates.com
Cover Design by Indigo Chick Designs

Prairie Spirit(s)/ Rhonda Parrish. -- 1st ed.

Physical - 978-1-988233-99-4
Electronic - 978-1-998563-00-5

Dedicated to my Patrons and to Jo.

Your support has meant the world to me.

CONTENTS

Introduction

In April 2021 the theme I'd given myself for Robert Lee Brewer's April Poem-a-Day challenge was 'Agrarian Decay' which I chose largely because I wanted to write about where I grew up in rural southern Alberta.

I've spoken frequently about the conflict I feel about where I come from–in so many ways I was a terrible fit for many of the people I was surrounded with growing up, but that hasn't decreased the connection I feel with the *place*. And as I sat down to begin this PAD challenge I was homesick (landsick?). I hadn't been any further from my home in Edmonton than I could walk in over a year because of a combination of the pandemic and problems with my right hip. So I was nostalgic and yearning and I thought I'd write about where I came from.

Perhaps I should have chosen 'Homesick/landsick' as my theme but I love the word 'Agrarian' and while looking for something to pair it with Decay just fit. So I thought, "Okay, let's explore this then… it's not exactly about where you came from, but it could be a fun filter to look at it through."

The first poems I wrote were full of frozen moments that included abandoned homes scoured grey by wind and time, wooden wagons with wheels buried up to the axle at the corner of a field and rusted out bodies of cars lined up in a row from oldest to newest. But it only took until day three before the first ghost appeared.

I invited it in, wrote about it (that poem eventually grew up to be "The Longest Journey") and then sent it on its way while I attempted another non-speculative poem about my chosen theme.

The next day some demons showed up–just sort of appeared fully formed on the page. I exorcised them from my brain to the page in a poem that eventually became "Relic" and tried to get back to my theme. Alas, then there were werewolves, and more ghosts… I got back to something non-speculative a few days later but even though it was rural it didn't fit my theme.

That's when I finally got it. The theme wasn't going to work. I wasn't writing about agrarian decay, I was writing about the prairies–about the spirit of the prairies as recalled from my childhood as I stewed in a very particular combination of nostalgia, sadness and homesickness, and also about fictional spirits which might inhabit that landscape.

I've gathered together some of the best examples of what I wrote for my new theme–Prairie Spirit(s)–into this collection, and tucked in a few poems I'd written before that also fit.

The resulting collection is mostly speculative (meaning it has elements of fantasy, science fiction or horror) but has some non-genre poems sprinkled throughout, as well as one or two which straddle the line between and can fully be interpreted either way.

Almost all of these poems are dark and many deal with death (including of children and animals) so they might be best taken in small doses with your shields in place unless, of course, you prefer stepping into the haunted house with no flashlight. To each their own.

Rhonda Parrish
Edmonton, Alberta
10/29/2022

How to Introduce Yourself to an Old House

Walk around her entirety,
appreciate her foundations
how long she has stood here
how much she has seen

Stroke her sides
watch the flecks of paint
fall, litter the ground
like lead-based snow

You mustn't stomp onto her porch
leaving muddy boot prints
nor rattle her door knobs
twisting and turning
like an adolescent trying to
"Tune in Tokyo"

Move slowly,
nearing her as a deer—
easily spooked and wary
—quiet as the dawn painting
her windows pink and orange
an echo
of the curtains she once wore

If her smile is broken,
pieces shattered by time
and children's stones
it is even more reason to be cautious—

she's been hurt before
she'll be slow to trust again.

Tread carefully upon her steps
respectfully across her boards

Slowly, slowly…

And knock before entering
because you never know
what waits inside.

Beneath

Leafless boughs
cast pallid shadows
across the snow

at the oak's base
Spring's breath
reveals twisted digits

curled into ashen claws
with the faintest hint
of chipped red polish.

Fifty-three

The winter of '53 was a beast
nothing so tame as a wolf at the door
rather a snarling, drooling monster
with eyes the colour of bile
teeth like a cultivator's
and a shaggy coat hung with icicles.

'Twas only when spring arrived
ice drip drop dripping into puddles
that become sloughs
and filled up the ditches
we learned that the impassible roads,
dwindling food stores and day after night
trapped with the same people
had turned men to monsters as well.

That Would Be Something

I don't believe in ghosts
but they believe in me
it seems.

At least I'm told that's the reason
my doors creak open
when no one's around,
and cold spots sprout
throughout my house
wild and random as the dandelions
which dot my yard.

The priest, whose religion I also
don't put much stock into
says I need to exorcise them
but I can barely be asked
to exercise myself
so that seems unlikely.

If only they could be trained
to do something helpful
water the plants, perhaps
or dust the tall shelves.

Now that.
That would be something.

Overheard on the Party Line

I know
I know I called before
but it's not a fox this time
officer Kelly
it's just not
foxes scream, true enough
but not names
they don't scream names
come as soon as you—

Foreshadowing

In April the water overflowed the banks
creeping out across the field
deep as my ankles
and then the rain stopped completely
not a drop since May
and the sun,
incessant, turned up to eleven
bakes the earth
dries the pond
I watch a water skimmer dance
over the surface
skating around the places a cow's skull—
a casualty of some other, long lost season
protrudes from beneath
more and more visible every day

Drought

The bones rattle together
clacking like dice but hollow,
hot and dry as an August wind
in his rough, work-stained hands.

Each sends up an individual plume
as it lands in the grey-brown dust
between his feet—bare as the fields
pressing down, deep down
into the earth to ground him.

He squints, shielding his eyes
from the relentless sun
with his hand
leans closer
while the crowd around him
murmurs in anticipation.

Most of the bones are from chickens
useless camouflage
for the three that matter
the three he acquired by moonlight
six feet down and covered in mud
those are the ones
who tell the story
a story of old gods distained
and their retribution
which will not end this day.

"No rain," he says
his voice the whisper of corn fields at night.
"No rain today."

The murmuring grows to a grumbling
and soon, soon
the bones say
it will grow louder still
until it becomes shouting
and flames
and sacrifice.

But not today.
Not for a while yet.
If they're lucky.

True Story

we smelled it first—
followed our noses
to the bloated remains
of a cow
her calf still half-protruding
(an apparent cause of death)

the maggot swarm they fed
was a thousand thousand creatures
and one
both at the same time

they writhed and twisted
splitting like the red sea
around the rocks we tossed at them
before melting around the stones
once more
unceasing in their movement
unrelenting in their feast,
their purpose,
beneath the early summer sun

Revival

He bumped into town
in a beat-up Ford truck
sand storm stripped of colour
and beaten down by the steady
tick tick tock of time

From out the back he pulled
yards and yards—an impossible amount
of dingy, once-white canvas
transformed it into a tent with
poles what stuck out the tailgate
twice as tall as any man

That night the lamp light
golden and warm as honey
cast a shadow play over the walls
poured out the door
and revealed the sandwich board sign
"Bertram's Tent Revival!"
it shrieked in garish red paint
which still showed the drip marks
from when it had been applied
too wet

The townsfolk filed in, two by two
each in their Sunday best
threadbare and well-patched
looking their most pious
their most righteous

Through the impossibly long, dark night
they worshipped and prayed
lifted their voices in song
and exultation of His name

In forty voices raised as one
they prayed for the rain
they prayed for the crops

they prayed for hope
and He heard their prayers

Hallelujah! Hallelujah!
and He came into their hearts
into all of their hearts
and He told them the price—
the price for their rain
the price for their crops
the price for their hope

With the dawn came the rain
which steamed where it struck the ground
like smoke rising from the earth
painting the world as a dream
edges blurred and lines unclear

It melted the tent like candy floss
plastered hair and clothes to shivering bodies
but though it washed the blood
from the hands of the thirty-nine still standing
it did nothing for their guilt
which would grow with the crops
and turn their bread to ash in their mouths
the profits to dust in their pockets

Hallelujah!
Amen.

Gopher Hunting

Driving an old beater through fallow fields
watching the boys take potshots
at any gopher unfortunate enough to
stick its head out of the hole to see what
all the ruckus was about.

I always wanted them to miss—
didn't want a single gopher to be hurt—
more than that I didn't want to be left out.

But if the car should unaccountably jerk
suddenly to the left,
throwing off their shot
surely that was down to a bump in the field
not the girl behind the wheel.

The Escort

Was it a crow or a raven—
the great bird, with oil slick feathers
which came to live with our chickens?
I was too young to tell.

It appeared one day and insisted on staying
with the hens when we locked them in
for the night
came out to wander during the day
and was back again by sundown.

As big as my baby brother—
who cried and cried
quieter and quieter
ever since the day they brought him home
from the hospital—
the bird, whatever it was,
hung around until the day of the funeral
and then I never saw it again.

Hush

I laze on the front porch
my creaky old chair rock, rock, rocking
while moonlight crawls across the lawn

every little blade of grass casts
its own shadow in the blue-white light
and crickets foolishly call out their locations
to the bullfrogs who sing in celebration
as they feast.

A wind shushes though the grasses
and reeds, ripples over the pond's surface
disturbing the reflection of a woman
long blonde hair drip drip dripping
and eyes empty as the old well
in the West quarter

I still the rocker, hold my breath
barely dare to blink.

No woman stands in the reeds along the shore

nor wades in the shallow, stagnant water.
No physical form, nothing from this world,
casts the reflection,
and I'll not be so easily caught as the crickets.

Poltergeist

at her graveside service we huddled
around a hole which seemed far
far too small for her
too small to contain her contagious laugh
her giant spirit of generosity
or her tornado of a temper

the grass, dead and brown crinkled
beneath my feet as I shifted one to the other
over and over
while the silence spread on and on
after the preacher asked if anyone wanted
to speak

but I knew—my whole family
staring down at our hands, at the ground—
we'd speak to her tonight
as we had every night since she'd passed
trying to coax her to the light or
at the very least
get her to stop breaking the dishes
as she raged against the unfairness of it all.

Relic

The salt shone, more blue than white
against the dark, loamy brown,
of the earth where I sprinkled it
I felt each grain as it passed
through my callused fingers,
tobacco stained and swollen
from the damp,
felt the sack grow lighter,
lighter
and lighter still.

I'd planned to use it on the fish
Gregory was sure to catch
when they were running in the fall
but what did it matter if we'd have enough
to make it through the winter
if we couldn't make it through
the night?

Inside the our dugout home
Goldie whimpered and cried
rattling the chain I'd used to bind
the fool thing
to the cold iron stove.
Friggin' dog wasn't smart enough to know
I was protecting her when, really,
I should chain her up outside
offer her as a sacrifice to Them
since the whole thing was her damn fault
to begin with.

Goldie had dug it up, whatever it was—
looked like wood
heavy as iron
carved with a bunch of foreign symbols
and when the twisted, broken shadow things
had surrounded the dugout
the damned thing had glowed a ghastly green
an evil green...

Praise the lord the house was dug
deep, deep into the hillside
with only one window through which
to look upon the world
or have the world look back

We'd lined the sill with salt
hung it with crucifixes
and prayed over it all night
as the things wailed
and shrieked
and beat upon it
upon the door
and the horse,
backed up against the inside far wall
stamped and snorted
and the dog, the damned dog, howled
and howled
and howled

They vanished with the dawn
melting back into the earth
like balls of tar tossed into a fire
sputtering and spitting

and Gregory rode out for the preacher.

But even if Gregory rode hard and didn't stop
not even for sleep
even then he and the preacher couldn't make it back
before sundown.

The sun crawled down
beneath the horizon
stretching the shadows across the prairie
and They drifted up out of the ground
like smoke—sulfur scented smoke.

I closed the door against them
as they amassed, boiling together
on the other side of the salt
their screams, their pitiful, horrible screams
clawing at my eardrums while the dog finally,
blessedly,
fell silent.

The salt line was thin but stretched
like arms wide open
across the entire front wall of our home
sealing off the threshold
buying me time.

It kept them back
held them at bay and
I breathed a sigh of relief
offered a prayer of thanks
just as the first bolt of lightning
painted the night sky

and the thunder rolled like laughter
across the prairie.

Minnows

we caught minnows in the creek
tossing in bits of bread
watching them crowd around it
nibbling and nomming until nothing remained
and then vanishing as quickly as they'd appeared
we'd scoop them up in a net—
actually a pair of stockings strung over
a curved coat hanger
but it did the trick—
and pour them into your little red sand pail
but when the afternoon was done and it
was time to go home
I said I was going to dump the pail out
releasing the fish back into the creek
like your mother told us to
but really I snuck one of the fish
the one floating still, silent on its back
into my pocket to take home
so I could bury it in my backyard
and dig it up later
and have a fish skeleton all my own

Gopher Season

Callused hands, nails bitten and dirty,
clutch a precious bit of bailing twine
looped into a noose-like thing.

Legs coiled like springs,
he crouches beside the dirt mound.
The loop of his "snare" arranged around the hole
just so.

The sun is hot on his shoulders
and the brown grass breaks
beneath his feet
when he shifts
but he waits
as still as he can
(though less than he imagines).

If he stays long enough,
quietly enough,
he'll see a head pop
out of the hole
and if he's fast enough,
he'll catch it.

He knows it.
Knows it as sure as he knows
the old Hayward place is haunted
and Santa is real.

After all,
didn't Billy's cousin's friend catch one

only two summers ago?

The Other Crisis

a bad football play
snap crackle popped his back
left him changed
damaged
broken

couldn't lead his team on the field
couldn't help his family on the farm
could hardly even walk
without quaking like an aspen
in Chinook winds

the pills helped a bit
a bit more if he took two
and on the days he crushed them
snorted them
on those days he felt like his old self
for a time

until two became four
became six
became twenty
traded for less and less time
as himself
his old self
or someone resembling him
anyway

kicked off the team
out of school
sent away by his family
to 'get help'
'get clean'
again and again
only to fail
again and again
and again

after the last stint he didn't come home
couldn't come home
couldn't see the pain his latest 'slip'
had added to their eyes

instead he moved
squatted some said
into the old Gottenberg farm,
falling down abandoned,
where he could be alone
with his habit
and its ghosts

where no one could watch
him fade further
fall one last time
and become a ghost himself

Winter Stores

The children raced through the hay bale maze
voices ringing through the golden day
giggles punctuating their parents conversations
where they gathered outside, sipping punch
swapping news, recipes and gossip—
the easy companionship of simple people
with simple lives.

The harvest had been good,
the best in a decade
but soon the snows would come
to blanket the world and isolate
them in their homesteads.

But that was a problem for another day.

Today was for soaking up the sunshine—
and each other's companionship
stockpiling it like the preserves lining the shelves
in their cold stores
so they'd have enough to get them through
the cold, dark days of winter.

Get Out

The windows rattled in their panes
as though thunder shook
but the sky was clear and blue
sun shining bright over golden fields.

Inside a room rank with the stench
of shit and vomit
lying on piss-stained sheets
straining against leather restraints
the shell of my mother writhed and flailed
spitting vitriolic hate, profanity and Latin.

My hands shook to hold the cross
while my father prayed
and my sister, Emily, rocked
back and forth
back and forth
in the corner.

Get out, Em whispered,
get out, get out, get out
louder and louder
until it became a scream which echoed
unendingly

the windows rattled in their panes
as though thunder shook
but the sky was clear and blue
sun shining bright over golden fields.

Forgotten Rake

Hides in the grass
awaiting your careless step
then smashing your face

The Longest Journey

Aliz crouched in the back of the wagon,
weather-beaten and grey,
the iron circling its wheels
orange-black
in contrast to the mellow gold
of the ripening wheat fields
all around.

A breeze stirred the sandy blonde
strands which had escaped
her ponytail
while the sun warmed her face
and the faded pink plaid button-down—
far, far too small for her—
which stretched
across her scrawny back
outlining every knob of her spine
as she leaned over
the board.

Alphabet crudely burned into the wood
the raw bit of wood lay ready
waiting

in the wagon bed before her
an over-turned baby food jar
meant to serve as her planchet
resting beside it.

Her pa would tan her hide
if he saw her here
like this
would beat her as bloody
as Ma had been the night
the baby came
late and backwards.

But Michael and Pa were both working
way up in the north quarter today—
so surely if she was quick,
if she was careful,
she could get this done
before little Izsak woke from his nap
before Pa knew she'd left him alone.

She had to do it.
She had to know.

Michael said someone had answered
when he'd tried last week
sworn it, sworn on everything that mattered
that they'd called him Mihály
like *she* used to

The glass was cool as the root cellar
despite being out in the sun
and her fingers gained halos of condensation

as she pressed their tips against it.

"Ma?" she said,
and her breath clouded the air
"Ma, are you there?"

And the jar began to move…

Waiting

The tattered scarecrow waits
rustling softly in the breeze
until a cocky crow ventures too near
and then he feasts

My Whole World

Spot's bark rings off the ice
sharp, excited,
bounces between the valley walls,
mingles with our laughter.
His nails clatter as he races
from one of us
to the other.
Fur streaming, tail wagging.

The blades strapped to our boots
cut lines beneath us
we twist, swirl,

swoop, twirl,
etching deliberate designs—
pretty frozen pictures.

Spot's tail smacks my frozen thighs.
Once, twice and again.
I rub the hurt with mittened hands.

Look, you cry, look at me!

You're poised like the ballerina painting
in our front hall,
tiptoe
balanced on the curve of your blade,
hands clasped together
over the pom-pom that tops your hat,
a perfect smile…

Then we hear it
soft but deadly
as an avalanche.

Spot barks,
crouches,
barks again.

Fear lights your eyes.

The spiderweb's center
between your toes
spreads, creeps toward me.

Spot dances back,

barking.

You tumble into the black,
icy depths,
without even a scream
and take my whole world with you.

Spooky Spencer

When I step into the shadows
of the twisted, old oak tree
all the sound goes away
like flipping off a light
no middle ground
no shades of grey
just light and birdsong
or shadows and silence

I tried to show my cousin
but he called me crazy
taunted me with the name
that name
all the kids at school use
"Spooky Spencer, Spooky Spencer!"

So I did the smart thing,
just stayed away from the tree
And when I noticed the shadow cast
by the pine outside his bedroom window
did the same thing
I didn't tell him

Didn't tell his parents when
a few weeks later
they found him
hair white as Miss Gracie's teeth
eyes wide as saucers
ice blue and unseeing
and unable to hear a word anyone said.

They wouldn't have believed me anyway.

In the Coulee

The locked river
cuts through the coulee.
Cobalt moonshadows stretch across
and pale blue light
reflects off the crystalline surface.

Beneath the trees,
evergreen but dressed in flakes
and clumps
which sparkle like stars,
the sentinel waits.

Antlers wide,
haloed in frozen breath,
still.

Winged thief casts a discordant spell,
steals the silence,
morphs the magic.

When its echoes subside
the guardian is gone
leaving only tracks.

Acknowledgements

"Beneath" was originally published on *Every Day Poets,* February 2013.

"Foreshadowing" was originally published in *Neon Magazine,* March 2022.

"Drought" was originally published on my Patreon, April 2021.

"True Story" was originally published by *Neon Magazine,* March 2022.

"Revival" was originally published on my Patreon, June 2022.

"Hush" was originally published on my Patreon, August 2021.

"Poltergeist" was originally published by *Star*Line*, March 2022.

"Relic" was originally published on my Patreon, October 2021.

"Minnows" was originally published in *Neon Magazine*, March 2022.

"Gopher Season" was originally published by *Fiction 365*, June 2013.

"Get Out" was originally published on my Patreon, May 2021.

"Forgotten Rake" was originally shared on my Patreon June 2022.

"My Whole World" was originally published on *Every Day Poets*, July 2013.

"Spooky Spencer" was originally published on my Patreon, March 2022.

"In the Coulee" was originally published by *Page and Spine* in December 2014 with the title, "In the Valley".

And Thanks

This collection probably wouldn't happen if not for my amazing Patrons:

7BitBrian
Aaron Clifford
AD
April Lydom
BD Wilson
Ben Asaykwee
Bobbi Styles
Brittany Warman
Cindy Gunnin
Diana Aitch
Diane Severson Mori
Emily Williams
Iseult Murphy
Joel Kreissman
John F Newsom
Kat Heydorff
Katie Rodante
Kirsten Lincoln
Krista D. Ball
Kristina Smith
Laura VanArendonk Baugh
Lloy Williams
Mark Carnelley
Mary Maceluch
Nds711d
Nikki
Riley
Sarena Ulibarri

SG Wong
Stephanie A. Cain
Steven Sparkman
Tammy Lee
Timothy Anderson
TinaFoo Spencer
Treena Davis

ABOUT THE AUTHOR

Like a magpie, **Rhonda Parrish** is constantly distracted by shiny things. She's the editor of many anthologies and author of plenty of books, stories and poems. She can often be found playing Dungeons and Dragons, bingeing crime dramas, making blankets or cheering on the Edmonton Oilers.

Her website, updated regularly, is at http://www.rhondaparrish.com and her Patreon, updated even more regularly, is at https://www.patreon.com/RhondaParrish.

DOWNLOAD MY AWARD-WINNING SHORT STORY FREE!

In this ever-changing world it is essential for authors to have a stable way to keep in touch with our readers so I have created a newsletter. It's a great way for me to touch base with you, let you know what I'm up to and share some freebies about once a month.

Please consider subscribing – I will even bribe you with a free short story!

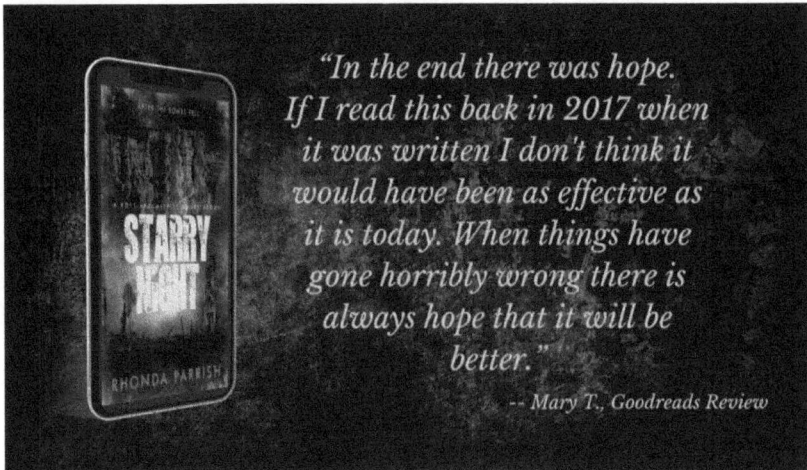

"In the end there was hope. If I read this back in 2017 when it was written I don't think it would have been as effective as it is today. When things have gone horribly wrong there is always hope that it will be better."

-- Mary T., Goodreads Review

"Starry Night" is an award-winning post-apocalyptic short story and you can download a free copy just for subscribing.

https://www.rhondaparrish.com/home/about/newsletter/

If you enjoyed this book please consider becoming one of my Patrons to enable me to create more of them :)

It is the only place a lot of my writing can be found and **includes almost everything I've published since 2019!**

Sign up for a free trial to see if it's a good fit for you, and if you decide to stick around tiers begin at just a dollar or two a month.

Check it out here:

https://www.patreon.com/RhondaParrish

SELECTED BOOKS BY
RHONDA PARRISH

HOLLOW
High school is horrible already, but what if we add a cursed
camera into the mix?

ONE IN THE HAND
Norse mythology-inspired urban fantasy

HAUNTED HOSPITALS
EERIE EDMONTON
Paranormal Non-Fiction

BLINDSPOTS
A talking animals story for grown-ups

SILVERSONG
Fantasy that will make you sad, but you'll like it

SELECTED ANTHOLOGIES BY
RHONDA PARRISH

FIRE: DEMONS, DRAGONS AND DJINNS
EARTH: GIANTS, GOLEMS AND GARGOYLES
AIR: SYLPHS, SPIRITS AND SWAN MAIDENS
WATER: SELKIES, SIRENS AND SEA MONSTERS

GRIMM, GRIT AND GASOLINE
CLOCKWORK, CURSES AND COAL
TRENCHCOATS, TOWERS AND TROLLS

MRS. CLAUS: NOT THE FAIRY TALE THEY SAY
UNTETHERED
HEAR ME ROAR
ARCANA
DARK WATERS

SWASHBUCKLING CATS: NINE LIVES ON THE SEVEN
SEAS
PIRATING PUPS: SALTY SEA-DOGS AND BARKING
BUCCANEERS

SALTWATER SORROWS

HAUNTINGS AND HOARFROST